THERE'S A TARANTULA IN MY HOMEWORK

by SUSAN CLYMER

Illustrated by Paul Casale

A
LITTLE APPLE
PAPERBACK

SCHOLASTIC INC.
New York Toronto London Auckland Sydney

ISBN 0-590-88025-X

12 11 10 9 8 7   8 9/9 0 1/0

Printed in the U.S.A.

First Scholastic printing, September 1996

To my family

1
The Cupcake Mystery

Micah sighed contentedly as Mr. Jenkins read the last page of *The Merry Adventures of Robin Hood*. Micah couldn't think of a more perfect activity for his ninth birthday. The teacher had read Robin Hood through all of January as whistling winds shook the windows of their third-grade classroom. He'd read the book through snowstorms and even an ice storm.

For probably the hundredth time, Micah wondered if Robin Hood had ever been a real man. Most likely, people had lived in

Sherwood Forest for a hundred years and all their adventures had been remembered together as Robin Hood. Micah folded his hands on his desk and rested his chin on them. That's how legends were formed — a little truth, a lot of exaggeration.

Micah closed his eyes and thought, *I wish that some day there would be a legend created about me.* Since last night, he'd been trying out different wishes so he'd be prepared when he blew out his birthday candles tonight. Oh, he didn't want to steal from the rich to give to the poor, like Robin Hood. He wanted to be something like . . . Micah Jacobs, the Environmental Wizard! Maybe he could be a journalist and write stories that would embarrass polluters so much that they would clean up the rivers and the air.

When Mr. Jenkins closed the book, the entire room stayed perfectly silent. That hadn't happened since Squeaks, their classroom hamster, had babies last fall in Mr. Jenkins' desk drawer on top of their spelling tests.

At that instant, the door of the classroom flew open, and the custodian stepped inside, carrying a large bag. The custodian was Micah's Aunt Grace. As usual, she wore a bandanna around her neck.

"The secretary said this bag had arrived for you from the pet store," Aunt Grace said to Mr. Jenkins, flicking the door shut behind her with one foot. "I offered to bring it down on my way to the gym." She waved two fingers at Micah.

Micah shook his pencil back and forth, in his secret greeting. This classroom was *not* on the way to the gym from the office. Ever since Mr. Jenkins had given Aunt Grace that giant chocolate bar as a reward for helping their class retrieve their wandering hamster on carnival night, Aunt Grace seemed to come by more often.

Aunt Grace swung the bag onto the teacher's desk, then peered into the top. Her eyes widened. "What in the world...?"

"It must be our new class pet!" Micah exclaimed.

"I certainly hope *that* never gets loose in my gym!" Aunt Grace announced, her hands on her hips.

Students leaped to their feet and raced to surround the teacher's desk. Micah squirmed into the second row. Before Christmas, their class had created a chocolate factory and had sold pretzels dipped in melted chocolate chips. Students from all over the school, even the *sixth*-graders, had come to spend their quarters. After the class had paid Mr. Jenkins back for his loan, they had chosen unanimously to use the profit to buy a tarantula! Mr. Jenkins had reluctantly agreed to have a new pet.

Now Mr. Jenkins gazed into the bag. His Adam's apple went up and down, so Micah knew he must be swallowing. "Jumping arachnids," Mr. Jenkins muttered, reaching very slowly into the bag. He pulled out a plastic jar holding the most striking spider that Micah had ever seen.

The tarantula had long brown fur all over its body. Down the middle of each leg

there was a darker brown stripe, surrounded by white. Tan stripes radiated out from the center of the top of the head, and it had black toes . . . though Micah wasn't sure that tarantula feet really had toes.

Several children gasped and stumbled backward. Micah stepped closer. After all, the spider *was* in a jar. It couldn't hurt anybody. Elizabeth stood right by his shoulder.

The spider's eight long legs looked like bent coat hangers. To his surprise, Micah felt goosebumps rising on his arms. He knew the tarantula wasn't poisonous, like in horror movies. Still, that hand-sized creature certainly looked as if it could destroy a mere boy.

Mr. Jenkins reached into the bag with both hands and pulled out the glass tank, lined with wood chips. A large rock sat in one corner beside a dish containing a wet sponge. The teacher held the plastic jar down in the terrarium and gingerly unscrewed the lid. Micah rose to his tiptoes to see better. The instant the lid was free, the spider scurried sideways out of the jar, highstepping with its legs, wiggling the spinnerets at the back of its eerie body. Mr. Jenkins hopped away with a muffled yelp.

Then the teacher hooked the lid back on the tarantula's home and slid the tank over next to the hamster cage on the corner of his desk. Squeaks lay sound asleep on her bed of cotton balls inside her little Lego house. She yawned, stretching.

"Mr. Jenkins, we shouldn't put the tarantula that close to Squeaks," Micah objected, remembering what he'd once read. "Tarantulas eat small rodents, like mice. Squeaks might be scared."

"Squeaks isn't a mouse!" Janna cried, rolling her eyes at her best friend, Elizabeth.

Mr. Jenkins crossed his arms and rested his chin on one fist thoughtfully. "It strikes me," he said, "that you all are going to have to thoroughly research your new pet."

The class moaned.

"Here it comes," David said.

Mr. Jenkins grinned. "In fact, I just got a marvelous idea. This will be the beginning of our spider unit. You can bring any type of spider from home. I know there aren't any alive outside since it's so cold, but you might be able to find spiders in your basement." He carried the tarantula's tank to the bookcase. Then the teacher patted his stomach and nodded at Micah.

It must be time for his birthday treats! Micah headed to the back counter and scooped up the tray his mother had left that morning. He handed Squeaks her piece of cheese first and gave a cupcake to his aunt and Mr. Jenkins. Then he neatly set a birthday napkin and a cupcake down on each desk. Yet when he got most of the way around the U-shape of the desks, he noticed that he was one cupcake short!

The students were bustling happily to their seats. "Yum!" Tom exclaimed, leaning over Micah's shoulder. He had the end desk. "Hey, don't I get one?"

Micah's heart sank down past his knees.

There had been twenty-three treats when he arrived at the classroom this morning — one for each student and two extra. He was as sure of it as his own name!

Before he could say anything, Aunt Grace slipped her own cupcake onto Tom's desk. Micah knew how much she loved sweets. "You saved my life," he whispered to her as his class started singing "Happy Birthday" in their off-key way. As Aunt Grace left the room, she scooped a piece of trash off the floor and tossed it into the trash can like she was shooting a basket.

"What's the matter?" David asked cheerfully at the end of the song. "Forget how to count?"

Micah ignored David's teasing. The class laughed, like they always did at David's comments. As Micah sat down at his desk, he realized something. Why, this was the second time this week the class had been one birthday treat short! Micah nibbled on his delicious cupcake. He was too careful a boy to have counted wrong, so that left only one conclusion. Someone must have stolen his birthday treat.

Stealing birthday treats was a dastardly crime!

Elizabeth had her head cocked to one side, watching him. Why, everybody knew that Elizabeth liked riddles and puzzles. She'd even started a detective company called Pipsqueak Detective Agency.

The other students chattered and laughed as they ate their cupcakes. No one acted suspiciously, like a thief. Micah's chest suddenly ached. Not a single boy or girl leaned across his desk to be friendly either. As usual.

Micah swallowed his last bite. Then he got an idea . . . an idea that seemed even more scrumptious than his cupcake. If he solved this mystery, his classmates might actually start to like him. They might think of him as a great guy.

Micah crunched up his cupcake wrapper. That's what he'd do, then. He'd take one small step toward becoming a legend.

2
The Astonishing Birthday Present

Micah closed his front door behind him. He didn't hear a single sound . . . not the stomping of feet carrying a package . . . not the rustling of wrapping paper. He'd hoped for a welcoming committee, maybe someone whistling "Happy Birthday."

Micah hung his backpack and jacket on his hook by the front door and headed up to Pop's studio. He peered carefully around the door jamb.

Startling his father when he was creating was *not* a good idea. Pop had been

11

known to jump and make a mistake in his painting.

Pop stood motionless in the middle of the room, staring at a painting on the easel in front of him. His head was cocked sideways, and he gripped the wooden end of his paintbrush between his teeth.

Micah couldn't tell what the picture was supposed to be about. It was one of those impressionist types with lots of swirls of color. "Hi, Pop," Micah said softly.

His father turned halfway and waved his paint palette at him, mumbling something that sounded like, "Welco ho." Pop seemed to have as much paint on himself as on his picture. He had orange and green dabs on his arms and face. The tips of his fingers were a watery blue color, and he even had purple paint on his forehead. His T-shirt said *Save the . . .* the last word, *Whales*, had been blotted out with green paint, as if he had been testing his paintbrush on his shirt!

Pop returned to his painting, his back

once again toward Micah. He hadn't even said, "Happy birthday." He must have forgotten.

Micah tromped down to the kitchen. He figured he had the oddest father in the whole world. He just hoped the other children at school never found out much about him. His strange Pop was his most private secret.

With a box of cheese crackers tucked under his arm, Micah headed to the basement to work on his train set. He had two big sets of tracks that circled under and around each other in figure eights. Micah had loved trains since he was about four years old. Every Christmas and sometimes on birthdays, his grandparents sent him a new car. Last Christmas, they had given him a special dual remote control.

Micah checked the alignment of the wheels on each car before he flipped the switch of the passenger train. The train chugged and clacked as it picked up speed. He liked the rhythmic sounds. The bars dropped and the lights flashed as the train came close to the road crossing. Then Micah started the freight train.

For the last six months, he'd been building a city inside the figure eights of track. He'd started with a train station made out of Legos. Then he'd created stores for the center of town. Next, he'd added five old-fashioned houses made from his castle kit. The train went through one of them. Recently, he'd built a giant log cabin for the art museum.

Micah plugged in the strand of miniature lights, and the houses glowed inside. He'd even made a row of streetlights, strung high on popsicle sticks stuck in clay. Holding his breath, Micah carefully stepped over a hurtling train. That always made him feel as if he were starting out on a journey. As the trains went whizzing around him, he crouched down to work on his clock tower. He hoped Mom would let him use her glow-in-the-dark alarm clock on top. Micah hummed, "I've been working on the railroad." As usual, he lost track of time.

"Don't you want to come upstairs for your birthday dinner?" Mom called from the kitchen.

Micah set his last miniature brick in place and drove his trains into their sheds. Then he raced up the stairs, two at a time. It was dark outside. Micah stopped at the bathroom to wash his hands. He tucked in his shirttail and buttoned the ends of his sleeves, looking at himself in the mirror. He combed his hair with his fingers. Something was missing. Micah ducked into his room, pulled his red bow tie out of his top drawer, and clipped it on the collar of his shirt. Now he was ready!

Mom whistled as he walked into the kitchen. "Wow, what a handsome young man!"

Micah grinned. Balloons hung down over the table and two presents rested on the floor by his chair. The one from the post office meant Grandma and Grandpa had sent a present! The other box was gigantic. Micah looked questioningly at his mom, but she was busy, or pretending to be busy, serving the mashed potatoes.

Just then, Pop sauntered down the stairs, still wearing his ruined *Save the Whales* T-shirt. Now his hair was sticking straight up, too. He did have a present in his hand, a flat one, perhaps a book on model railroading. Pop set the book on top of the two boxes. "Happy birthday, ten-year-old son!"

"Nine," Micah corrected.

His father smiled serenely and gave him a hug.

They sat down to a dinner of meatloaf and mashed potatoes — his favorite, mouthwatering, meal. Still, Micah ate quickly. The family rule was that you couldn't open your presents until dinner was finished.

Mom seemed particularly cheerful, talking about her morning delivering a baby. Her favorite part of being a doctor was bringing new life into the world.

By the time Micah ate his chocolate cake

with maple icing, he could hardly stand the suspense, even though he loved the sweet taste. Pop had pulled a pencil from his back pocket and started drawing on his napkin.

Micah opened Grandma and Grandpa's present first. Inside the tissue paper lay a new caboose, from the Santa Fe line. Wow! At last he had a caboose for his freight train.

Next, Micah reached for his father's present. Pop looked up from his drawing. One could never be sure what Pop would give as a present. Last year, he had given Mom three different types of bugs for the garden, announcing that they would eat pests.

Micah pulled off the funny papers. Inside lay a book called *Sketching for the Young Artist*. Micah opened it to a page that showed how to draw a dog, using circles. He tried to look interested, but he had never once in his life sketched anything.

Pop slapped him gently on the shoulder. "Every boy needs his own sketchbook!"

Micah straightened his bow tie.

"Thanks." He had no idea what to do with this. Well he could give the book to Elizabeth at school. She liked to draw. That thought made him blush.

Micah reached for the third present. Mom always gave the best presents. He scooted the heavy box out into the middle of the floor, then crouched to rip off the paper. The box lid said *Hobby and Lumber*.

"Lumber?" Micah asked, puzzled.

With a pleased giggle, Mom leaned over and slit the top of the box with her jack-knife. Micah yanked open the box. Inside lay pieces of lumber, and piles of bolts and washers. Micah pulled out a wheel. "What *is* this?"

His mother looked a bit like a cat who has just swallowed the family cockatoo. "A soapbox derby kit," she answered. "It's for both of you."

Micah went over in his mind the images he'd seen in the newspaper of boys and girls zipping down a steep hill on wooden carts,

wearing helmets. Their fathers usually stood nearby, cheering.

"A car, Bubeleh?" Pop asked, astonished. "Bubeleh" was his nickname for Mom. He dropped his sketching pencil.

"This will be good for you," Mom insisted. "A project for you two to do together. The competitions start next spring. So you have plenty of time to build the car."

"Competition?!" Micah stared at his mom, his mouth falling open. He didn't much like competitions. That's why he didn't play on the boys' soccer team. And he liked to build with little blocks, not hammers and saws and screws. Besides, Pop never did any of the things that most fathers did with their sons. He'd never taught him how to ride a bike, or even play baseball. Now they were supposed to build a car together! Micah couldn't imagine it.

Mom served them each an extra piece of cake. "I'll do your cooking this weekend so you can start on the go-cart," she said, squeezing Pop's shoulder. Pop always did the cooking on the weekends. That's when Micah noticed that his father's mouth was hanging open, too. His face looked pale beneath the purple spots on his forehead. Mom had shocked him speechless!

Then Micah realized that for the first time in his whole life he would be doing something that would make the other boys in his class green with envy . . . most of the girls, too. He knew for sure that Tom would love to build a car. He was almost as interested in racing cars as he was in ballet. Yet the idea of spending time with his father was already making him nervous. Micah could hardly swallow his peppermint ice cream.

Mom kissed him lightly on the top of the head. "Happy birthday, Micah," she said mischievously. "You are well loved."

3

The Tricky, Sticky Web

"The Sticky Webs!" Elizabeth exclaimed. She'd been drawing a spiderweb in one corner of their giant construction paper envelope. Micah, Elizabeth, Janna, and Tom had pulled their desks together out of the U-shape so they could work as a spider research group this Friday afternoon.

Micah had just finished writing. "Most baby spiders crawl up to a high place after they are born. They spin a web and let the wind blow them to their new home. The spiderlings sail like a balloon in the breeze." Micah slipped the piece of paper into their envelope.

Now he peeked at Janna's fact: "A male spider can become a tasty snack for a female if he's not careful."

That made Micah shiver, and shivering reminded him of his *secret* plan. Since no one had had a birthday lately, he couldn't solve the cupcake mystery. So he'd created a desperate plan on the way to school this morning. He had gone through nine long years and three days of life without being popular. Today was the day for a change!

"The Sticky Webs should be the name of our spider research group," Elizabeth repeated.

Janna chewed on the end of her pencil. "We can give ourselves spider names, too. I'll be Dr. Janna Web."

Tom smiled. "I'm Arachnid Tom."

Micah swallowed. Now he had to come up with a name. He looked over at their motionless tarantula for inspiration. He could be Sleepy Tarantula. The spider lifted one long leg and waved at Micah. No, it was the spider's hair that was so special. "I'll be Hairy Micah Tarantula, the third," he announced.

To his surprise, the others laughed and nodded. Micah couldn't remember a time when his classmates had thought he had a good sense of humor. Maybe he should enter the name "Hairy" in the classroom's tarantula-naming contest.

Their teacher had decided they should turn their room into a spider display for open house. Right now, Mr. Jenkins was balanced on a ladder, adding a quote to their spiderweb bulletin board. Micah read the words to himself: "We did not weave the web of life. We are merely a strand in it. Whatever we do to the web, we do to ourselves . . ." by Chief Seattle.

Chief Seattle was a famous Indian who had lived hundreds of years ago. Micah liked the quote. It reminded him of the Native American legend of Grandmother Spider creating the world. Everything in the world was part of her web, even the people. She was a great trickster and liked to catch the four-leggeds — the animals — and the two-leggeds — the people — by surprise when they were being especially foolish.

"Web of life!" Mr. Jenkins exclaimed, hopping down off the ladder. "I lost track of time. Change stations, spider students."

Micah hurried to the back table. Now the Sticky Webs got to build their giant spider! The class was creating huge arachnids that would hang from the ceiling. The first step was to blow up big balloons for the two body parts, the abdomen and cephalothorax. Then they had to cover the balloons with three layers of newspaper dipped in the bucket of gooey flour and water. Once the papier-mâché dried, the spider would hold its shape even if the balloon popped.

Micah blew up a red balloon and carefully tied it off. He was just about to set it gently on the table by the bucket of flour paste when he decided this would be a good moment to begin his secret plan.

Now?! a part of his mind yelled in the background.

He'd never done anything like this in his life. But he was willing to try almost anything to get the kids to admire him. Instead of setting the balloon down, Micah poked it on purpose with his cufflink.

BANG! The balloon popped.

Tom jumped, and Elizabeth glared at him.

"Do you have to be so clumsy?" Janna whispered.

Mr. Jenkins waved the rest of the class back to work, then said in a kindly way, "Try again, Micah." The teacher was helping Anna draw a crab spider.

Micah frowned. Well, that certainly hadn't worked. Yet David did this sort of thing all the time. He showed off and all the kids liked him. Micah was determined not to give up.

This time, Micah blew up an even larger balloon. Desperately, he tried to think of what he could do now. Popping the balloon hadn't made everyone get excited. How about, instead of tying the balloon off, he let the air out slowly?

But . . . how would David go about this? Micah tried to imagine the other boy in his head. David would dance around. Micah knew he wasn't so good at dancing around. But he could jump on his chair. That would make him more obvious. Without giving himself another second to think, Micah stood up on his chair. He stretched the mouth of the balloon sideways and let the air seep out. The balloon made a raspberry sound . . . a *loud* raspberry. The whole class turned to look. Micah raised the balloon higher over his head. He even kicked his feet like he was dancing.

Elizabeth stared at him as if she'd just seen a horse in the classroom. That almost made Micah stop. He cared about what Elizabeth thought. Yet the entire class was beginning to giggle. He couldn't quit now.

"Micah?" Mr. Jenkins straightened to his full height, astonished.

The entire class roared with laughter. Micah twirled on the chair, delighted. His plan was working! Now the kids would really start to appreciate him, just like David. Showing off wasn't so hard for a shy boy after all. He should try this more often. The balloon kept making a high-pitched raspberry sound. Micah twirled harder, still kicking out with his feet. His right foot accidentally slammed against the bucket of flour paste on the table. The bucket spun around once and tipped.

Tom gasped and dived for the bucket.

The bucket crashed over in slow motion, splattering all over Micah's legs and the table. The class fell silent as the sticky flour and water mixture dribbled down the chair and formed a messy pool on the floor. Mr. Jenkins looked extremely irritated. In fact, he looked like a volcano about to explode.

Micah stopped twirling. He hadn't meant to cause a mess. His black pants were wet and sticky from the knees down. He held one foot up in the air. Into the sudden quiet,

Micah exclaimed, "Oh, no! My new pants are filthy!"

The laughter in the class started up again. Only this time the students weren't enjoying his cleverness, they were laughing *at* him. They often teased him for caring about being clean. Mr. Jenkins didn't usually allow teasing, but today he wasn't interfering.

Micah's ears started burning. His plan to be admired had seemed to be going perfectly, and now it had turned into a disaster. His legs felt horrible and sticky, almost as if he'd been caught in one of Grandmother Spider's tricky webs.

Mr. Jenkins brought a rag over and dropped it on the table in front of Micah. "You have *totally* disrupted this class."

Micah saw, in utter dismay, that the teacher held Stuffy in his arms. Mr. Jenkins pretended to be the giant stuffed rabbit and said in a high-pitched voice, "Wait! I'm sure there is something else going on, maybe even something bothering

the youngster. Micah is always such a well-behaved boy."

"Well." Mr. Jenkins looked at Stuffy, then back down at Micah. He cleared his throat more gently. "Do you want to tell me what this is all about now or during recess, young man?"

Micah scrubbed at his pants leg. "Recess, please," he mumbled. Right now, he wished he could turn into a spiderling and crawl through one of the cracks in the ceiling. He'd spin a web on the school roof and balloon all the way to China. And he'd never *never* come back.

4
Go-Carts and Coal Cars

Micah and his father leaned over the blueprints, their shoulders touching. Pop's fingertips were purple, and there was a rather dashing blue streak across his cheek this Saturday morning.

Micah picked up a bolt and turned it over in his hands. They had just figured out that his present wasn't really a soapbox derby kit. It was more like a simple go-cart. So far they had identified the two by fours, square flat pieces of wood for the seat, and four wheels. That flimsy rope was supposed to be for steering the cart!

"Just like building a picture frame," Pop muttered for the third time.

Micah dragged the two by fours to a clear spot in the garage, arranging the matching ones about four feet apart as the axles. Then he stretched the longer piece between the two axles. This frame didn't look strong enough to hold up a chicken, let alone a sixty-two-pound boy.

As Pop started drilling a hole through the middle of the front axle, Micah wrapped his arms around his knees and day-dreamed. He imagined himself putting on his helmet, listening to the announcer calling out his name to a cheering audience. "Micah 'Speedy' Jacobs, ladies and gentlemen, the undefeated cart racer for all of the Midwest. Our own home-born famous LEGEND!" The audience roared. Micah hopped into his car with a skillful jump, and he was off! He raced down the hill, zipping around the turns. . . .

"Micah," his father said, a bit grumpily.

Micah scooped up a long bolt. The washers and nuts and screws were supposed to be *his* job. Micah knelt down by the front of the go-cart, trying to follow the instruction in the diagram.

Pop had been moody lately. Last night at dinner, Pop had announced that a fast food restaurant had offered him a contract to paint wall-sized paintings for buildings across the country. The problem was that Pop wanted to paint ART. They'd had one of their two-hour dinner conversations, about how art should help people see beauty in the world, not sell hamburgers.

Micah slipped a washer onto the bolt, then pushed the bolt through the hole that Pop had drilled in the frame. Next, he put on another washer; no, two of them. He shoved the bolt through the front axle. Hey, this wasn't much harder than building with Legos. Micah looked up, exclaiming, "Pop, I'm doing it!"

His father sat at the back of the go-cart busily drawing. He seemed to be sketching a little picture of Micah on the axle.

"Pop!" Micah cried, watching his father draw glasses on the picture and add a few strands of hair sticking up in the back of the head.

"Oh," Pop said, flushing, as if he'd just realized where he'd been drawing. "Sorry."

Micah watched his father's cheeks turn red. He thought he was the only one in this family who did that. Micah tightened the nuts. He didn't want his father to be embarrassed. "Oh well," he said, trying to make Pop feel better, "drawing on a go-cart is better for the environment than using up paper, right? Save trees, draw on your go-cart!"

Pop's quick grin made him look handsome, in a Robin Hoodish way . . . particularly with that rakish blue streak across his cheek that looked like a sword swipe. He picked up the power drill. Sawdust flew in all directions as Pop drilled the hole in the rear axle.

Suddenly, Pop's eyes changed. For the first time in his life, Micah saw the change as it happened. Pop's eyes took on that shining look he always got before he shut himself in his studio for a week. Micah held his breath as his wild-eyed father set the drill down.

"Recycling!" Pop muttered as he put the cart seat in place on the frame.

Micah started screwing in the rear bolt.

"Composting!" Pop whispered. Then he chuckled gleefully, "Using hamburger wrappers as drawing paper!"

Micah figured that today he must have the strangest father in the *universe*, not just the world. Pop held the seat steady while Micah pounded in the nails. The seat back was straight up, rather than slanting as in the picture. Still, this was really beginning to look like a cart! Next weekend they could add the wheels and the steering rope.

Mom came out with a batch of cookies just as they finished working on the frame.

"We have a genius for a son," Pop announced. "He gave me the idea for using an environmental theme for the art for the fast food restaurant."

"I did?!" Micah said, wiping the dust off his knees. All he'd done was make a joke about drawing on go-carts. Still, Micah didn't mind being called a genius, not one bit.

Pop squeezed his shoulders. "Now I'll be able to enjoy doing the project. Who knows, perhaps I'll even influence the company in a humorous way to help the environment."

While Pop explained his idea, Micah grabbed six chocolate chip cookies, three in each hand. He wasn't supposed to take more than two, but his parents were too busy talking to notice. "Thanks for your help, Pop."

Micah skipped upstairs to his bedroom. He lifted his teddy bear hamster, Wiley, out of his cage. Wiley was Squeaks' son and had been born last Thanksgiving at school. The teenage hamster tried to nibble his cookies.

"Chocolate chips are *not* good for you, fellow," Micah said, carrying the hamster inside his shirt as he tromped downstairs to his train city.

Micah put on his blue-and-white-striped engineer's hat.

Wiley usually explored while Micah worked on his train city. Today, the greedy little chewer kept climbing up Micah's pants leg to get at the cookies. On a whim, Micah lifted the hamster into the coal car of his freight train and turned the train onto its slowest speed.

As the train chugged around the first turn, Micah smiled, thinking about how the morning had gone. In real life, not just in a daydream, he and Pop had spent two hours together and gotten along. He'd even had fun!

The teddy bear hamster stood up and faced forward, resting his front paws on the roof of the next car. By the second round, Wiley stuck his head out of the top. His golden bushy fur blew back from the sides of his face. Too bad Wiley didn't have a tiny engineer's hat. Micah laughed, delighted. Why, his hamster looked for all the world as if he were driving the train!

5
Being Brave

Micah took a running jump and slid on the snow through the back gate of Martin Luther King, Jr. Elementary. He had gotten to school early. To his surprise, he saw Janna crouched by the Dumpster, petting the homeless cat.

The kindergartners, including Micah's cousin Natalie, had named the skinny cat Trashtruck. All the students in the school were trying to keep him a secret from the custodian.

Micah scooted into the building without

Janna seeing him and slipped into the empty classroom. Mr. Jenkins must be down in the teachers' lounge. What luck! Micah slipped off his heavy jacket, headed directly to the tarantula's tank, and lifted the lid.

He had come up with another idea for his *secret* plan to get his classmates to appreciate him more. He wanted to show them he was brave. Unfortunately, the only brave thing Micah could think of to do was to pick up the tarantula.

As usual, the spider rested motionless by its rock. Micah reached into the tank very carefully. Last night, he'd reread his spider book so he could do this safely. He spread his thumb and index finger like pinchers and held them above the tarantula's body.

Micah pinched the fingers together in slow motion. The tarantula's fur felt silky. It woke up and scooted sideways.

"Sorry, Hairy," Micah whispered. He'd already entered "Hairy" in their spider-naming contest. Micah reached for the tarantula again, pinching more quickly.

His heartbeat picked up speed like one of his trains as he lifted the tarantula out of the tank.

Holding his breath, Micah set the spider down on his goosebumpy arm. His book said that tarantulas couldn't bite anything as big as a human. Still, a nervous tarantula would kick its abdomen hairs out with its back legs. The sharp little hairs would enter a person's skin and itch like crazy.

Micah held completely still while the tarantula crawled up his arm. It felt . . . gentle. Hairy lifted each leg high into the air and set it down on his arm. Micah smiled. He even started to breathe again.

"What are you doing?" a voice hissed at his shoulder.

Micah jumped. Elizabeth stood beside him, looking like a cross between an angry thunderstorm and a worried cat.

Micah didn't blame her. But he wouldn't hurt Hairy. Micah put his free hand on his upper arm above Hairy and the tarantula crawled onto his knuckles. The little sticky

pads on the ends of its legs tickled. He held Hairy out to Elizabeth. "Want to hold our tarantula?"

Elizabeth gasped. She glanced at the door, then reached for the spider. Micah watched Hairy high step from one of her small hands to the other. Once, Hairy clung to her hand and hung almost upside down, but didn't fall.

Finally, Elizabeth held the tarantula back out to Micah, her face transformed with joy. She truly loved animals. Micah quickly transferred the tarantula into the terrarium. Hairy scurried over to the rock.

"You're a private sort of a creature, aren't you?" Micah asked softly. Then he added to himself, "Just like me." He couldn't show off shy Hairy in front of the class just so he could look brave. That wouldn't be fair. Micah sighed. He'd just have to come up with a different idea for his secret plan.

Elizabeth twisted the latches closed on the lid. "How's Wiley?" She had one of the hamster babies at home, too.

The tarantula had frozen into perfect stillness again, playing invisible spider. Micah figured that the tarantula believed that if it didn't move, nobody could even see it. "Wiley learned how to drive my train this weekend," Micah said proudly.

"What train?" Elizabeth asked.

"I've got two model trains and fifty feet of track," he replied.

"Could I see Wiley drive your train sometime?" Elizabeth asked. "Please?"

Mr. Jenkins walked into the classroom. "Silk Streamers!" he called. "Isn't this a great day?"

Micah had no idea how to reply. He felt as frozen as the spider. His feet wouldn't budge. "I . . . I'll think about it," he managed to mumble.

After a normal Tuesday morning of math and library, Aunt Grace stuck her head in the classroom. "Happy Presidents' Day!" she sang out, then slipped a container of treats onto the back counter. "See you twenty minutes before the end of the day."

Mr. Jenkins' eyes lit up, and he licked his lips.

"Zekes, treats for Presidents' Day!" Anna exclaimed.

Everyone looked at Micah, while he tried not to turn red. What was Aunt Grace doing? Luckily, all his classmates seemed to think she had brought the treats because of him.

Micah spent most of the lunchtime wondering what he would do if he invited Elizabeth home. He didn't think she'd like go-carts. And what if she met Pop?!

Next to him, David cut up his sandwiches into insect shapes, so he could pretend to be a garden spider, and catch his prey in an orb web. He had brought in a garden spider this morning that his father had found miraculously still alive in her greenhouse.

After recess, the class voted on spider names in a secret ballot. Their choices were Hairy, Fang, Tula, Sticky Feet, and Brownie. The student who thought up the winning name would get to take the tarantula home for a weekend.

Finally, it was time to work on their giant spiders. The Sticky Webs had decided to make theirs into a trapdoor spider. Mr. Jenkins stood on Janna's desk to hang the huge arachnid from the ceiling. It was nearly as big as a third-grader! Then Micah held the spider book and pretended to be a theater director, showing Tom and Elizabeth exactly where to paint the markings.

At ten minutes before three o'clock, Aunt Grace sailed into the room. She wore her red, white, and blue bandanna knotted around her neck, the one she saved for patriotic holidays. Micah gaily waved his pencil at her. As the students started putting their desks back into the U-shape, Aunt Grace delivered the treats. They were huge cookies decorated like tarantulas and smelling like applesauce. Yum!

Suddenly Micah saw his aunt freeze. She looked down at the container in her hand, then back at the students. Micah could tell she was counting.

Counting?! Did that mean . . .

"I'm afraid," the custodian announced, "that one cookie is *missing*."

Mr. Jenkins already had his mouth open for a big bite. "That's the third time we've been one treat short." He set his cookie down, giving them all his fiercest look. "Is there a thief in my room?"

Micah gripped the corner of his desk. Someone must have taken the cookie during lunch or recess. He tried to remember who'd been missing. Anna and Jack and Tom had stayed inside to finish their stories. Janna and some of the other girls had gone to the bathroom, but he hadn't kept track to see who had come back quickly.

"Since it's Presidents' Day . . . do you all know the old story of George Washington and the apple tree?" Aunt Grace asked. She flushed when David giggled. "I mean the cherry tree. Remember, young George cut the tree down. When he was asked if he was responsible, he said, 'I cannot tell a lie, I did it.' "

"So . . ." Mr. Jenkins stood up to his full height. "Who is stealing the treats?"

No one responded.

Micah felt his conscience prickling him — as if waving a flag in his mind, telling him there was something he should do now. "Aunt Grace," he said, rising, "Tom can have my treat." Micah very reluctantly slid his cookie onto the last desk.

"Now you saved *my* life!" Aunt Grace whispered, breaking her own cookie in half to share with him.

Mr. Jenkins sat down with a thump, a bewildered look on his face. "We have a problem, children, that we *will* discuss . . . tomorrow. For now, I can't interfere with this lovely party offered by such a thoughtful lady." He gallantly bowed his thanks to the custodian.

When the bell rang, the students filed out of the classroom. Squeaks sat on top of her cage as she often did, watching them go, accepting little pats on the top of her head. Janna sneaked her an extra sunflower seed.

Mr. Jenkins motioned Micah to come up front. Micah swallowed. The teacher didn't think he had stolen the treats, did he? "You won the naming contest, Micah," Mr. Jenkins said. "Ask your parents if you can bring Hairy home this weekend."

Elizabeth was waiting outside the door for him. "Next week," Micah said breathlessly. "Come over to my house Tuesday." And before he could change his mind, he turned around and ran.

6
Flying Hairy

"Remember, you're a giant to Hairy," Micah warned, trying very hard not to lose his patience. Natalie darted her hand inside the tank and stroked Hairy with one finger, like she'd been told. She still managed to flatten the poor tarantula.

Hairy waved his spinnerets and darted sideways. Micah firmly latched the lid in place. Natalie was the most maddening six-year-old he had ever met. Worse than that . . . she was his cousin!

Hairy stalked toward one of the crickets

Mr. Jenkins had put in the tank. The tarantula lifted its legs high above its body and crept closer to the prey, just like a cat.

"Time for dessert," Mom called from the kitchen.

Micah trooped downstairs. His cousin skipped beside him. "I have to go to the bathroom," Natalie announced. She zipped back upstairs, rather than using the one on the main floor. Micah shook his head. He had given up long ago trying to figure out his younger cousin.

Aunt Grace wore a pretty blue dress and no bandanna. Since she couldn't dress up at school, she often did at home. Aunt Grace motioned Micah to sit on the couch. "Here's your strawberry Jell-O."

Natalie trotted back down the stairs, her left hand holding the railing and her right hand in the pocket of her jumper. She smiled at her mother, then slipped Micah's birthday present from the coffee table.

"Where's Pop?" Micah asked.

"Painting," Mom replied.

Disappointed, Micah took a nibble of his Jell-O. He had to admit it tasted great. Natalie sauntered over to hand him his present.

"May this gift lift up your wheels," Aunt Grace said with a lopsided grin.

What a puzzling clue! Micah carefully balanced his Jell-O bowl on his knees, holding the present above it. He ripped off the paper. Suddenly, something *scurried* around the side of the present, right onto the top. A long-haired, eight-legged creature stared at him eye to eye. The giant tarantula rose up onto his back feet and waved its front legs at his nose.

Micah gulped. He could see the spider's pink fangs on its black underbelly. They looked like little lobster pinchers, sharp and vicious. It was going to bite him!

Micah couldn't help himself. He tossed the present in the air, jumping to his feet with a yelp. The tarantula went soaring. It sailed up up . . .

"Flying tarantula!" Natalie screeched, delighted.

Aunt Grace gasped in pure shock. Micah turned away from the sailing spider to see strawberry Jell-O splattering all over his aunt in red splotches. "Bother," Aunt Grace exclaimed as another blob of Jell-O came down right on her head and the bowl landed in her lap.

At that moment, Micah realized that the tarantula had to be Hairy. But where had the poor guy landed? What if he were hurt? Tarantulas were fragile! Why, Hairy could have even broken a leg.

With a furious shout, Micah pounced on his cousin. "How *dare* you take Hairy out of the tank?" He knocked Natalie down and sat on her. He'd never in his life done anything like this. Natalie pounded on his chest with her fists, then burst into tears.

Mom grabbed Micah under his arms and hauled him away. "Micah!" She sounded appalled. "You are too big to behave this way!"

"No one could be a bigger sneak than Natalie," Micah yelled, then started searching the room for Hairy. His heart seemed to stop beating as he looked on the couch and on top of a lamp. No Hairy.

Aunt Grace sat Natalie firmly on the couch. Natalie squeaked but didn't say a word. No one argued with Aunt Grace when she was feeling fierce.

Micah searched behind the curtains as Mom bit her lip and peered under the chair. "Come here, little tarantula," she whispered, then shivered.

"I'm sorry, Mikey," Natalie said in her most angelic voice.

Micah examined the bookcase. Still no Hairy. He wished he could feed his cousin to some very hungry polar bears.

"I'm sure Hairy will come out when he's ready," Aunt Grace said, trying to sound cheery.

Micah opened his present in stunned silence, while Aunt Grace sat on one side of him, dabbing at her face with a washcloth.

He unwrapped a super duper bridge for his train. Micah leaned his head on his aunt's sticky shoulder. "Oh, Aunt Grace," he said and then realized he was about to burst into tears. She patted his leg.

Micah clutched his bridge to his chest and stumbled upstairs. He shut himself in his bedroom and sat on his desk by the empty tarantula tank in worried silence, tears trickling down his face. Even the two crickets had gotten loose.

Micah hardly moved until he heard the rest of his family going to bed. Then he sneaked downstairs and searched every nook and cranny for Hairy. He half expected the tarantula to drop down onto his shoulder in the eerie darkness. When the living room clock finally struck midnight, Micah dragged himself to bed . . . all alone.

7

A Tarantula Baby-Sitter

Micah opened one blurry eye to see his father leaning over him. "Out of bed, lazybones!" Pop exclaimed. "Time to build." Micah blinked. Pop had never come to wake him up before. What was going on?

Pop pulled Micah into a sitting position. "If your pet tarantula were dead, we'd have found the stinker by now," he said. He scooped a cricket off the windowsill and dropped it in the tarantula tank. "Hairy will turn up sooner or later, hopefully not in your mother's medical kit."

Micah pulled on his only pair of jeans and a sweatshirt. Poor Hairy. He followed Pop down the stairs. Mom had loud classical music playing in the kitchen while she drank her coffee. Micah checked the curtains and window ledges for a creeping brown furry spider.

Before he was truly awake, he had eaten his blueberry bagel and found himself out in the garage, watching Pop attach the wheels to his go-cart. Micah drilled the holes and secured the steering rope himself. Then they attached the brake and even the seat belt. Nothing was left in the box except three washers, pieces of cardboard, and two little blocks of wood.

"What are those for?" Micah asked.

"Beats me," Pop said, examining the diagram one last time. He handed Micah his bicycle helmet. Micah sat down in the cart. He felt about two feet tall, he was so low to the ground. Pop ceremoniously pushed him out of the driveway. Then he turned the go-cart so that it faced straight down the hill.

"Uh, Pop?" Micah said. His street suddenly looked like a mountain.

Pop must not have heard, because he gave him a grand running push.

Micah zoomed past the neighbor's driveway. As the wind blew against his face, he felt excitement burning inside him like a candle. "Hurray!" he yelled.

Only . . . now he seemed to be veering toward the right, aiming directly at a parked car! Micah pushed with his right foot and yanked on the steering rope with his left hand as hard as he could. He wished he had a third hand so he could pull the brake lever.

With a sickening screech, the cart went into a twirling skid. Micah spun round and round. To his horror, he spun off the street and up the Johnsons' driveway. The go-cart crashed sideways into a tree.

For an instant the whole world went black. Micah's chest hurt with a fiery heat. He couldn't breathe! But then he could see Pop racing down the street toward him, wide-eyed with worry. His father ran up

the driveway and knelt beside the cart.

"Micah?" Pop held his head and stared into his eyes. "Are you hurt?" Then he muttered, "No concussion."

Micah found that he could pull air into his lungs again. "Just dizzy," he admitted. "Is . . . is the cart supposed to do that?"

Pop unstrapped Micah's helmet, then pulled at the tear in his jeans so he could see better. "Nasty scrape." He unhooked Micah's seat belt and watched grimly as Micah crawled onto the ground. "Enough is enough!" Pop exclaimed. "Do you like all this go-cart stuff?"

Micah rose to one knee and put his hand on Pop's shoulder. "I like being with you," he panted, honestly, as he stood up. Ouch, his knee stung, and his elbow was bleeding.

His father put his arm around him. He held up the blueprint, then suddenly hit his forehead with the palm of his hand. "I bet the chunks of wood in that box are these safety blocks that limit the steering angle. No wonder you went into a spin."

Pop grabbed the rope of the go-cart, and they started up the street together. Pop leaned his head down closer. "We built the go-cart like your mother suggested. Now, let's do something *we* both like." Pop waved at a neighbor. "Any ideas?"

Micah shook himself all over to clear his foggy mind. He absolutely couldn't imagine Pop building with Legos or driving a train. "My train city," he blurted as he stumbled up the driveway. "Will you paint me a backdrop on the basement wall?"

"On the wall?!" Pop exclaimed, dropping off the go-cart in the garage. "Son, your Mom would fry us!" Pop opened the back door. "Let's go upstairs and find a canvas."

They tiptoed into the house together. Micah was so astounded to be sneaking in with his father that he didn't even care about his bruised knee and his aching shoulder. Mom sat in the living room reading the paper, but she didn't notice them.

They crept up to the bathroom first to clean his "honorable wounds," as Pop called them. Then they raided Pop's studio.

Micah balanced a tray of paints as they hurried down to the basement. He could hardly keep from giggling.

"Wow!" Pop exclaimed at the bottom of the stairs. "You've put a lot of work into this. I should come down more often. What do you want? A cityscape or a cloud scene?"

"City, please," Micah answered, "with lots of tall buildings." He felt bold, so he added, "And clouds in the background."

Pop grumbled good-naturedly, then roughed out the picture on the canvas with a few deft strokes of his pencil.

They spent the next three hours together, just the two of them . . . like any father and son. Micah built his clock tower and every once in a while gave his father an eensy suggestion about his painting. It was absolutely the best afternoon Micah could remember in ages.

After dinner, Micah limped upstairs to his bedroom. His knee had started to stiffen during dinner. Today had been the best of days . . . and, Micah had to admit, the worst, too. None of his family had seen a single sign of Hairy, not one hair.

Now, it was Sunday night. Micah imagined the scene at school tomorrow: When he arrived without Hairy, everyone would be sure to surround him. They would want to talk to him. But they certainly wouldn't admire him very much. Perhaps he should pretend to be sick? Or maybe he could tell Mr. Jenkins that Hairy had gone to live in the desert? Micah sighed.

He had failed as a tarantula baby-sitter!

Micah hobbled over to feed Wiley a sunflower seed. Then he pulled out his desk chair. He had a book report to write for tomorrow. He'd spent the last week reading *The Indian in the Cupboard*. Failing to do his homework would not help this stomach-twisting, no . . . hair-raising situation.

Micah lowered himself gingerly into his chair. His desk was a total mess. Micah rummaged around looking for a pencil.

Oooh, his right elbow was beginning to bruise and turn an icky shade of green. Soon it would probably be purple. Oh well, Mom had checked him over and said he would heal in a day or two. She didn't even seem too upset that he and Pop had given up the go-cart for now and switched to painting. All she really cared about was that they do something together.

Micah cleared aside the top papers. His report form had to be in this stack, somewhere. The stack rustled. No, that was just his imagination . . . or the mess. He didn't usually let things get like this. He moved another paper.

Four feelers with sticky little black feet on the ends waved at him. Micah stared, astonished. Standing right on his book report form was Hairy! This time he didn't jump in surprise. Micah yelled at the top of his lungs, "Hey, Mom! Hey, Pop! There's a tarantula in my homework!"

Both of his parents came running. His mother arrived holding a stethoscope. She must have been checking her medical kit. His father had a paintbrush in his hand.

Pop patted Hairy. "How did you climb the stairs, little guy? Are you a magical spider?" He left a little bit of red paint on the tarantula's abdomen.

"No, he's just a smart spider!" Micah exclaimed. "He knew to come back up here to *me*." Micah let the tarantula crawl all over his arm. Hairy did seem glad to be with him. He didn't have any injuries that Micah could see. Just in case, Micah held the spider out to Mom. "Will you check him over?"

"No thanks!" she said. "I'm a doctor to humans, not arachnids!"

Micah slipped the spider into the tank with the lone cricket. "We've both had a busy weekend, Hairy." Micah lifted the tank onto his desk so he could keep one arm around it. "Let's just do my homework together."

8
Elizabeth Visits

To Micah's surprise, his tongue and mouth worked normally when he walked home with Elizabeth on Tuesday afternoon. They talked about the continent she had made up for creative writing called Spiderica. "Spiders weave castles out of webs there," Elizabeth explained. "And Spiderica has spider-shaped lakes."

"I'm home!" Micah called as he entered the house. He always went right up to Pop's studio to check in, but not today. Hopefully, Pop would be too busy to notice.

Micah hadn't said a single word to his parents about Elizabeth's coming to visit. When Mom had dashed off to deliver a baby this morning, he had moved Wiley's cage down to the kitchen so everything would be ready.

"Want some juice?" Micah asked, releasing a sleepy Wiley from his cage and plunking him on Elizabeth's shoulder. He balanced two glasses of apple juice and a box of cinnamon graham crackers as they headed down to the basement.

Elizabeth stopped so suddenly on the bottom step that Micah bumped into her and hurt his sore elbow. He'd been wearing a long-sleeved shirt that covered the bruises.

"Wow! You must have spent months building this!" Elizabeth exclaimed. Micah nodded, pleased. "But . . ." She pointed at the backdrop. "I didn't know you were such a good painter!"

He should have known she would be interested in artwork. "Pop paints."

Elizabeth tilted her head to one side,

resting her cheek against Wiley's fur. She looked curious. "I've never heard you mention your father." Wiley cleaned his face with his little paws, preening.

Quickly, to change the subject, Micah showed Elizabeth how to set Wiley in the coal car. She patted the teddy bear hamster as Micah turned on the train. Chug, chug. Chug, chug. Once again, when the train reached the first turn, the little hamster stood up in the car.

"Hurray for Wiley, the train driver!" Elizabeth cheered loudly.

"Ahhh," Pop said, leaning his head around the basement door. "I thought I heard *two* voices." Pop strolled down the stairs. A purple flower was painted on his jeans, probably as a practice design. He wore a Christmas T-shirt . . . in February! Worst of all, his shirt pocket was full of cold, ugly french fries.

Micah suddenly wished he could crawl into a hole. Instead, he squeezed his eyes shut. Tomorrow at school, Elizabeth would

tell all the other kids about Pop. Micah could imagine them all laughing and pointing at him. Everybody would point at him. He would be teased forever . . . *forever!*

"Your backdrop is really marvelous, Mr. Jacobs," Elizabeth said politely.

Micah opened one eye. Elizabeth seemed to be *smiling* at his father.

Pop ruffled his hair back and left a streak of blue paint in his bangs. "Would you like to see some of my paintings?" He turned on one scruffy tennis shoe, waving over his shoulder for the children to follow him.

Micah knew his lower jaw must have dropped all the way down to his own shiny black shoes. Pop *never* shared his artwork until he had finished.

Upstairs, Elizabeth hesitated at the doorway to the studio. Then she tiptoed in as if she were entering a museum, her hands folded behind her back. Elizabeth stopped in front of the impressionist painting on the easel. "Such bright colors," she breathed.

"Want to be an artist?" Pop asked.

Elizabeth stared up at him, as if he were a magician. "How did you know? How *could* you know?!"

Pop tugged her braid gently. "I can recognize the longing, that's all."

Micah felt amazement creeping into his chest as he watched the two of them. He'd never in his wildest dreams imagined that Elizabeth and his father would like each other *this* well. Elizabeth walked around the room, gazing at the drawings tacked to the walls. Most of the drawings had little hamburgers and french fries. That must be why Pop had french fries in his pocket, as models. Micah joined her. He hadn't seen this fast food series yet.

"Sketches for murals," Pop explained. "That one will be in Chicago."

Elizabeth stood on her tiptoes, then pointed to the little girl in the corner dropping a hamburger wrapper into a huge recycling box. She giggled. "You sure can draw, Mr. Jacobs."

Now Micah could feel another emotion in

his chest, starting in a cold jealous lump and growing outward. Micah clapped his hands together. "Wiley! We left him riding on the train." Micah turned and ran downstairs as fast as he could go.

To his relief, Elizabeth followed him. As they reached the first floor, the front door slammed. "I'm home!" Mom called. She had her back to the two children, hanging up her coat on a hook. "What a hard day I had, delivering that baby!"

"Mom," Micah warned.

Mom went right on speaking. She loved to talk. "Robert finally came out, safe and sound . . . if a little red." She chuckled. "He burst into life feet first, Micah, just like you."

Micah froze in embarrassment.

Mom twirled around with her arms outstretched for a hug and saw Elizabeth. "Oh! Hello."

"This is Elizabeth," Micah croaked.

Mom smiled charmingly. "Welcome to our home." She glanced at Micah, lifting her eyebrows. He could tell from her teasing expression that she was about to get back at him for not mentioning Elizabeth's visit. "Would you like to stay for supper tonight, Elizabeth?"

Micah choked. He couldn't help himself. So he pretended to sneeze to cover up.

"Wouldn't that be nice, Micah?" Mom continued. "We have plenty of spaghetti." Elizabeth bounced happily from foot to foot.

The palms of Micah's hands started sweating, but he knew when he was trapped. "Sure," he muttered.

Elizabeth called home. "Good!" she said, hanging up the phone. "I get to eat a dinner without my two-year-old sister, Hillary."

Then they hurried down to the basement to rescue Wiley, but the hamster seemed perfectly happy, riding around and around. Micah could imagine him waving each time he sailed by. "My pet is a train fanatic," he said.

"Just like you." Elizabeth crouched down in the middle of the zooming trains. "You don't have any statues in this city."

He rather liked having someone help with the building. The singing sounds of his mother's Mozart symphony swirled around them. Just as Micah finished his hotel, Elizabeth leaned over a zipping locomotive and poked his shoulder. "You should bring your trains to school so everybody can see this."

Micah looked up. "We're studying spiders. Trains don't have a thing to do with spiders."

"Oh, Micah," Elizabeth said, exasperated. "Why are you so . . . so serious all the time?"

He didn't have an answer for that.

"Dinner!" Pop called.

Elizabeth set her statue of an airplane on a pedestal. "I bet you a million dollars, a million dollars of Monopoly money, that the kids would love your train city."

Micah stood up, his hands on his hips. He meant to exclaim, "I couldn't!" But instead he said, "You think they would?"

His mouth seemed to have a mind of its own these days. Micah had never thought of sharing his hobby with his classmates. He brushed off his knees and straightened his slacks to hide his nervousness. "Would you . . . will you help me ask Mr. Jenkins?"

"Sure," Elizabeth answered, then she exclaimed, "Bet I can beat you to the table!" She raced up the stairs.

Elizabeth shared Micah's side of the dinner table. There was plenty of room for two, and she was much more fun than Natalie. Elizabeth spun her spaghetti on a fork rather than cutting it up like his family. She laughed at Pop's recycling jokes and chatted with Mom about Mr. Jenkins. When Micah kicked her foot under the table, she tickled him back.

Right after dinner, Mom drove Elizabeth home so that they would both have plenty of time for their homework. Micah hopped out of the car and raced Elizabeth to her front steps. This time he won.

Elizabeth didn't open her door. "You

have such fun parents, Micah. I wish . . ." She sighed softly. "Oh, I wish I had a dad like yours."

Micah stepped back, startled. Elizabeth wished she had a father like *his*?! Couldn't she see that Pop was messy and wild-eyed? That he was totally unpredictable? No one ever knew what Pop would do next! Why, sometimes he would disappear into his studio and hardly come out for a week. Then Micah remembered. Elizabeth was adopted, and she had a mother and a sister — a fine mother and sister — but no dad.

Suddenly, Micah felt a great bravery growing inside him, much greater than when he had picked up the tarantula, or even when he had offered Tom his cookie at school. He took a deep breath and firmly banished that hard lump that had grown inside his chest this afternoon.

"You can share my pop anytime," he said and gently swatted Elizabeth's shoulder. Then he ran to his car, yelling, "See you tomorrow at school!"

9
Two Hairys!

Micah surveyed his classroom with pride. Yesterday after school, Pop, Elizabeth, and even her mom had helped him set up his trains. They'd had a smashing time, as Pop said. Aunt Grace hadn't been able to resist setting aside her broom to help. Micah's train sets and city now filled the entire reading circle. The spider pictures from *Charlotte's Web* swayed above it all.

Since Elizabeth had visited his house a week ago, Micah had been busy. He'd created a new street of elaborate paper homes, with mailboxes and dogs.

During that week, the class had had another birthday, and, of course, they had been one treat short. Mr. Jenkins was so upset that he'd started a unit on Honest Abe. Micah wished he had some real clues to help him solve the mystery. He flipped the switch for his freight train, and then, the one for his passenger train. The trains picked up speed together. Too bad Wiley couldn't be here. The two trains crossed over and under each other in a whirling pattern. Whistles hooted and lights flashed.

Elizabeth came in and stood by Micah's shoulder. "I knew you'd be here early today." Micah didn't answer, but he grinned.

Just then, David came dashing through the classroom door. "What's *that*?!" he exclaimed, good-naturedly.

One by one, the other students entered and surrounded Micah. As usual, Janna was the last one to arrive. "Who built this town?" she asked, tossing her hair over her shoulder.

"Micah did," Mr. Jenkins replied. "He hasn't shared anything for show and tell all year, so I let him bring in his train set."

"Micah?!" Janna exclaimed.

Micah rather liked hearing the amazement in her voice. He figured he had surprised lots of classmates today. Micah showed them how his trains worked and how he'd built the different types of houses. "Can we see if Squeaks will drive the freight train?" he asked at the end.

"Who ever heard of a hamster driving a train?" Janna exclaimed in her most sarcastic voice. She rolled her eyes.

Micah laughed. "Wiley drives."

Tom came up behind Micah, punching his arm. The arm didn't hurt anymore from his go-cart crash. "Good job, Hairy Micah Tarantula, the third," Tom whispered. "You're getting us out of morning drill."

They usually did math problems and sentence punctuation for the first half hour of school. "Anytime, Arachnid Tom," Micah replied, poking his fellow Sticky Web. This was the first time he'd played around with Tom. It felt good.

Mr. Jenkins lifted a sleepy Squeaks out of her cage and set her down in the coal car. Her little fat body barely fit. Micah turned on the train to its slowest speed. Instantly, Squeaks puffed to twice her normal size, as if every hair on her body were sticking out. Her eyes widened.

Before Micah could flip off the switch, the hamster leaped out of the chugging train. She scurried up and over the Lego train station and disappeared beneath the bookcase.

"Wow!" David exclaimed. "A vanishing hamster. Say, why don't we let Hairy drive?"

Micah knew Hairy was too fragile to drive the train, but everyone turned to look up at Hairy's tank on top of the bookcase. Then Micah stiffened and gasped, at the same moment as every other kid in the room. Hairy lay on his back with his stiff legs straight up in the air!

"Our pet's dead!" Janna wailed. Elizabeth moaned. The two best friends put their arms around each others' shoulders.

Micah's heart slipped inside him. He crossed his arms over his aching chest. Then Micah remembered a picture he'd seen in his spider book. Suddenly, he wasn't sure Hairy *was* dead. "Maybe not," he whispered.

Elizabeth was the only one close enough to hear him. She narrowed her eyes at Micah. "What do you mean?" she asked, but he wouldn't answer.

Mr. Jenkins took off his glasses. "Just to be on the safe side, no one touch Hairy until I have time to call the pet shop."

In the middle of science class that afternoon, Micah's suspicions began to come true. It started when he saw Squeaks come out and sit down on top of the bookcase close by Stuffy, as if for reassurance.

Next, Micah saw the "dead" tarantula

begin to wiggle. Micah got shivers up his spine, but he didn't say anything . . . not until Hairy seemed to be pulling a leg out of his skin. "Mr. Jenkins!" Micah pointed at the tank.

The class watched the transformation in astonished silence. Finally, Hairy crawled away to sit on top of his rock. His skin stayed behind. The shed skin looked exactly like another tarantula.

"Hallelujah, two Hairys!" Mr. Jenkins exclaimed.

"I have an idea," Micah said. With the teacher's permission, Micah put the shed skin in the coal car and turned on the freight train. Sure enough, it looked just as if a tarantula were driving his train!

The students cheered and pointed. Micah looked around, delighted. Even the teacher laughed until his face looked as red as a cherry.

"What do you think, spider students?" Mr. Jenkins asked. "Perhaps this train should remain in the room as part of our spider open house next week?"

10
The Open House

For Micah, open house nights always felt special, a little mysterious. During the day, reading and writing seemed . . . so normal, but at night, learning took on a magical quality.

Pop, tall and scrubbed clean, stood beside him near the trains. Micah had the delightful feeling that his father felt proud to be standing at his side.

Mom was across the room, reading his acrostic poem with Elizabeth's mom. They had instantly liked each other so much that

Mom had invited Elizabeth's whole family to dinner next Saturday. Pop had even offered to cook. Micah didn't mind one bit.

The classroom slowly filled with parents admiring the children's work. A sign over the door said *Enter the Web*. Parents had to duck so they wouldn't hit their heads on giant hanging spiders.

A large group had gathered around David's garden spider, commenting on its beautiful orb web. Others read limericks that were taped on the windows. The fact envelopes were propped against the walls.

Most of the kids said hello to Micah as they circled by. He couldn't believe how much his life had changed. Once he'd stopped playing invisible spider, like Hairy, his classmates seemed to like him just fine. All he'd had to do was to let them see a little bit of who he really was. His trains had done the trick.

The classroom was getting hot. Micah grabbed a cupcake and headed outside to be alone for a few moments. He couldn't believe the silly things he'd done to be popular . . . like showing off. He stepped out into the crisp cold darkness. He was so glad they had studied spiders. Without the creeping critters, his life never would have changed.

Micah sat down by the Dumpster. It had all started with Hairy. Good old Hairy. Who could imagine that a tarantula could change your life? Micah unwrapped his cupcake and took a bite, a giant *peppermint* bite. As he was swallowing, he heard a soft voice on the other side of the Dumpster. "Come on, Trashtruck. Poor little cat."

Micah crawled closer, curious. Who would be talking to Trashtruck at night?

"Doesn't butter frosting taste good to you?" the voice pleaded in that false high tone that some people use with animals or little kids. The cat mewed.

Micah stuffed the rest of the cupcake in his mouth and soundlessly crept around the side. The kindergartners had noticed that Trashtruck had been getting fatter.

"Tubby, tubby, tubby," as Natalie had said. Micah couldn't tell who was talking, but he had an adventurous feeling growing inside of him . . . as if he were about to make a discovery.

"Doesn't anybody else feed you?" the voice asked. "Don't worry, I'll keep bringing you treats."

Keep bringing you treats?! Micah thought. He sprang out of the darkness, yelling, "Thief!"

The cat let out a sharp cry and vanished into the darkness. Micah had one glimpse of a fluffed-up tail as it passed under a light. Micah didn't land on the thief as he'd expected, but he did grab a handful of a jacket. The jacket struggled.

"Mr. Jenkins!!" Micah yelled at the top of his lungs. He needed reinforcements. "Elizabeth!" he called.

Panting, he dragged the struggling thief back into the hallway outside his room. That was the first time he got a good look at her. "Janna!"

Janna had frosting on her hand and there were cupcake crumbs on the front of her jacket.

Elizabeth burst out of the room and came to a standstill in front of them.

"What are you doing to my best friend?!" she demanded, glaring at Micah.

"She was feeding Trashtruck our treats," he replied quietly, letting go of Janna's jacket.

"Janna?" Elizabeth sounded shocked. She reached out, then let her hand fall.

Janna gave them both the meanest look she could. Yet when Mr. Jenkins pushed his way out of the classroom, followed by her parents, Janna burst into tears. "Trashtruck didn't have anyone else. He was starving," she wailed. "I've been stealing from the rich and giving to the poor."

"Just like Robin Hood," Micah whispered.

Janna nodded.

Mr. Jenkins put his arm around Janna's

shoulder. "Oh, Janna, that's no excuse for stealing."

"But, Robin Hood did it," Janna cried. "And he's famous! And you have to admit our class is *rich* with treats!"

Micah remembered seeing Janna sneak Squeaks extra sunflower seeds every chance she could. She had a soft spot for animals. And thinking of being a legend like Robin Hood could make you get sort of carried away with yourself. Micah looked back at the classroom door and saw how many students had crowded around. Even some of the parents peered out from the doorway.

In that moment, Micah knew exactly how embarrassed Janna must feel. She wasn't the only person who had done some foolish things lately. "Help me," he said to Elizabeth. Janna and her parents and Mr. Jenkins still had a lot to talk about.

Micah lifted his hands up and waved everyone back inside the room just as he'd seen the teacher do. Elizabeth shut the door firmly behind them.

"And now for the big train show!" Micah exclaimed.

Elizabeth gave his elbow a squeeze before she pulled away. "You're a great guy, Micah Jacobs," she whispered, "even if you did solve the mystery before I did!" Then she called out, "Have you all seen the giant spiders?" As if anyone could miss them.

Micah turned on his trains, and explained over and over again about how Hairy had shed his skin. Pop stayed right beside him. Ages seemed to pass before Janna came over to him. "I get to keep Trashtruck," she said.

Micah stared at her. Somehow that seemed like a reward for stealing.

As if she read his mind, Janna sighed. "I also have to write a three page report on Honest Abe. I have to apologize tomorrow to every person in the class and your aunt Grace. Last but not least, I have to make you all an extra special set of treats." Janna smiled as she tossed her hair back over her shoulder. "Want to help me catch the cat?"

Micah shook his head. He'd done enough leaping in the dark tonight. He saw Elizabeth going outside to help her. That's when Micah noticed that the room was nearly empty. He took a deep breath and sank down to sit on the floor by his train controls.

He'd caught the thief.

His father didn't seem like the oddest man in the universe anymore. Micah grinned up at Pop, still talking to another parent by his backdrop.

"Bye, Micah Hairy Tarantula, the third," Tom called.

And he'd made a few friends . . . just by being himself.

There was no doubt about it. This was the best of all evenings. Why, this might just be the best night in his whole nine years.

Micah flipped off the switch and watched the lights stop flashing, the whistles stop tooting, as the trains came slowly to a stop.